Wolves, Humans, Dogs & Civilization
and how that happened!
Revised, March 2023

Stephen Hall

Wolves, Humans, Dogs & Civilization

Copyright © 2023 Stephen Hall

All rights reserved.

ISBN: **9798388632937**

Wolves, Humans, Dogs & Civilization

DEDICATION

To my late wife, Wendy Hall, who inspired and educated so many folks to continue her process of rescuing wild animals in need, rehabilitating them and releasing so many of them back into the wild. I'd also credit the Wildlife Refuges of America and Canada, especially Yellowstone, Algonquin Provincial Park and the Adirondack Mountains of New York, and to my favorite authors and virtual teachers, L. David Mech, Rick McIntyre, Rolf Peterson, Curt Stager, Nate Blakeslee, Cristina Eisenberg, Barry Lopez, Christopher Ketcham, Stephen Herrero, Rick Lamplugh, Jim and Jamie Dutcher, Marc Bekoff, Farley Mowat, Bill Bryson, Yuval Noah Harari, Jared Diamond, Bill McKibben, Nigel Calder, John Muir, Teddy Roosevelt, Aldo Leopold, Edward Abbey and many others.

Wolves, Humans, Dogs & Civilization

Wolves, Humans, Dogs & Civilization

CONTENTS

	Introduction	i
1	Wolves	1
2	Wolves, Humans, Dogs & Civilization	Pg 39
3	Public Lands, Ranching & Wildlife	Pg 78
4	Rewilding the Adirondacks	Pg 94

Wolves, Humans, Dogs & Civilization

INTRODUCTION

Why are human beings the dominant species on earth? How could a hominid barely 300,000 years old have come out of Africa, and despite being less robust than Neanderthals, and with a brain case smaller than theirs, not only have survived as the only human, but spread our cultures all over the globe, and moved from tool making to religion, to understanding the universe in terms of science, and developing technology to master and ultimately threaten nature itself? Could we have had help from another species?

Are we making the most of our shrinking American landscape, or are our imaginations and our futures held captive by old myths, prejudices, and political privilege, in which most of our land is used to produce foods which are less and less healthy for us, as we continue to push nature out of the way, in a blind race to see whether we can survive as a species? Do we really care about the world we leave our children and grandchildren, or will we continue with a mad consumer driven culture in which the future is someone else's problem?

Looking to our local economy, the Adirondack Mountains of New York, where tourism is clearly the most contributing part of the economy, and yet we draw an insignificant portion of tourist money spent in the state, should we broaden our attempts to draw tourist dollars with winter sports, hiking and camping, and aim to become the Yellowstone of the East, sharing the wealth with smaller communities beyond Lake Placid, Lake George and Old Forge? If the Adirondack motto is "Forever Wild", what can we do to restore much of the wildlife and wilderness lost, and what factors might enable that?

Stephen Hall
Adirondack Wildlife Refuge
March 2023

Wolves, Humans, Dogs & Civilization

1 WOLVES

Kiska, 7 yr old female gray wolf at Adirondack Wildlife Refuge, by Terry Hawthorne

Wolves are like us in ways we admire, and like us in ways we wish we were not.

Few animals have been as romanticized and vilified as wolves have, but after five decades of observing and studying wolves and moose on Isle Royale National Park in Lake Superior, researchers Durward Allen, Rolf Peterson, L. David Mech, John Vucetich and their teams, have greatly enriched our understanding of wolves.

Subsequent studies in Yellowstone, along with thousands of hours of wolf watching by retired Park Ranger Rick McIntyre, and his band of "Wolf Watchers", along with video documentary maker Bob Landis, has helped us better understand the lives of gray wolves, their family pack structure, and their impact on habitat as keystone predators.

Wolf Watchers in the Lamar Valley in Yellowstone, by Steve Hall

While our nearest genetic relatives are bonobos, a type of chimpanzee, whose family tree we split from 5.5 million years ago, there are many other ways to look at mammals, and I believe the closest family structure to humans is not a primate, but the gray wolf.

The Wolf Pack

Wolves, like all wildlife, most particularly in northerly climes, are subject to the conditions and extremes of the seasons, which control the life cycles of wolves. The core of a wolf pack consists of the breeding male and female, often referred to in the past as "alphas", who generally turn out to be "Mom" and "Dad", and the "pups of the year", anywhere from four to seven, who, following mating in February, are born about 60 days later, towards the end of April or in early May.

The other members of the pack are mostly older siblings born the previous two or three Springs. You'd better not be small when winter returns, so wolf pups are physically mature in terms of size by the time they are 8 or 9 months old, but not sexually mature until sometime between their second and third year. Females usually reach sexual maturity before the males.

Throw in the occasional straggler absorbed or dispersed from another pack, who often fill a functional need, sort of a job opening within the pack, and you have a wolf family, curiously similar in structure to a human family, but greatly modified by seasons and how difficult it is to make a living in nature.

Red Wolf Pups from US Fish and Wildlife, public domain.

Pups are born blind and deaf, weighing about a pound. They have little sense of smell and are barely able to crawl. They have a good sense of touch and taste, which helps them locate one of Mom's eight nipples, where they'll suckle for three or four minutes four or five times over 24 hours, while Mom's body heat keeps the pups warm. Their heads are comically oversized and rounded, with small ears and pushed in snouts, along with disproportionally large paws.

They remain in the natal den, often a narrow burrow with

twists and turns and both entrance and exit, dug out of a sun exposed hill, or a natural cavity or shelter just large enough to fit mom and her pups, and any visiting support wolf, until they're about four weeks old, at which time they begin emerging from the den. A breeding female may maintain multiple dens, for use as backup, should the natal den be compromised by other females, intruding members of another pack, or natural causes such as collapse or flooding.

Wolf Den, https://www.flickr.com/photos/usfwshq/14682953521

When first open, pup eyes are bluish, gradually transitioning to shades of yellow to orange, beginning at about two months old. Their eyes can detect light, but shapes are fuzzy and indistinct. They begin to stagger up on all fours and topple, stand and topple. Pups weigh about four pounds at a month old, the floppy ears have just about straightened out, and initial attempts at howling begin.

Like the young of other predators, wolf pups are eaten up from nose to tail by curiosity, and prone to wander, so as they grow, at about three lbs. a week, Mom may have one or two adult wolves or older siblings from previous Spring litters serve much of the time as pup sitters, who try to corral the pups into a manageable space, while discouraging any curious bears, coyotes or other potential predators from approaching. As the pups begin weaning, Mom takes advantage of the presence of sitters by going on some hunting forays of her own.

When the pups are about a month old, their hearing improves, they get better command of their bodies, and dominance play begins. They may begin to follow adult wolves on an ever-increasing circle of exploration around the den, sometimes up to a mile away.

Older siblings and other pack mates, along with Mom and Dad, protect the pups of the year. Whelps in the process of weaning may obtain food by approaching and nuzzling or licking the muzzle of any mature wolf, which then regurgitates undigested food. After a few weeks of such behavior, the pups' jaws have become strong enough to eat chunks of meat.

At about 4 months of age the pups are led to kill sites to feed and begin learning the ways of adults. When the denning season ends, the family tends to gather, eat and socialize at "rendezvous sites", which may be where the last kill was made. By the time the pups are six months old, they resemble slightly smaller adults.

Wapiti wolf pack near Tower Junction in Yellowstone, Nov 2017, with Rick Macintyre and Bob Landis, by Steve Hall.

Like most predators who go after large dangerous prey, and contrary to our impressions of predators in popular culture, wolves would greatly prefer discovering freshly deceased prey, rather than risking their lives attacking animals which defend themselves quite effectively.

Wapiti wolf pack near Tower Junction in Yellowstone, Nov 2017, with Rick Macintyre and Bob Landis, by Steve Hall.

When it comes to eating, the pack pecking order favors those wolves best suited to providing food for the others, usually the alphas, but not always. The best elk killer in the pack might be a beta male or female. In either case, the pack will need them next week, when they are starving again. Omega wolves are pack members who may be able to provide for themselves, catching rodents and small mammals, but not as likely to provide a surplus for the rest of the pack to enjoy. They likely eat last, unless they have a higher member in the pack, providing for and protecting their interests.

Mature wolves do sometimes take an interest in paying attention to, playing with, and protecting pups and juveniles who are subjected to bullying and ostracizing during the rough play process of approaching adulthood. Higher ranking wolves will play with youngsters, even sometimes pretending that the young wolves are "winning" in mock competition with their elders.

Four to seven pups are a lot of mouths to feed, and wolves are forced to go after larger, more dangerous prey, such as moose, elk and bison. Using Bruce the Moose as an example, moose are extremely dangerous in defending themselves, and wolves test twenty moose for each one they decide to attack. What are they testing?

For starters, any obvious physical disability, lack of mobility, or perhaps the wolves are smelling open sores and wounds, but I believe there's more going on than just that, and I further believe that the development of dogs as medical surrogates is demonstrating what's really happening. Dogs have demonstrated that they can smell tumors in their owner's body, can be taught to smell the correct amount of insulin in a diabetic, and whether a patient has cancer or not.

If we extract from facts on the ground, and since we know that dogs are genetically wolves, with a wolf's keen sense of smell, it follows that wolves may be smelling the presence of diseases such as CWD (chronic wasting disease), jaw necrosis, brain worm, heart disease, cancer and arthritis in the moose.

Zeebie, 3 months old, by Terry Hawthorne, Soul Expression Photography.

Wait a minute! Are we claiming that wolves know what cancer is? No, but just as human beings are primarily visual in orientation when it comes to sense experience, and just as we have a huge store of visual memories, and can envision past experience, so your dog, being a wolf, depends very heavily on olfactory evidence which may mean that wolves can associate the smells of disease with past hunting experiences, what a particular scent indicates, and what has worked and what has backfired in the past.

As young wolves enter puberty, their desire to mate may prove disruptive and trying to the rest of the pack. While brothers and sisters seem to have a natural aversion to mating with each other, there have been father daughter couplings, and in any case, the youngster needs to weigh the desire to mate, with the dangers of dispersing from the relative safety of Mom and Dad's territory.

They may seek to fill a position in another pack, or find an area where the pressure from resident, territory defending packs is diminished, or where they may start their own pack with a dispersing or wandering member of the opposite sex.

This leads some young wolves to disperse up to 600 miles away from their natal pack, and explains how wolves spill over into adjoining areas, such as Minnesota wolves spreading to Wisconsin and the upper peninsula of Michigan. Now and then, the over-abundance of prey animals such as deer, will result in larger packs, where more than one pair of wolves is mating.

Wolves lead very dangerous, risk-prone lives, and any wild wolf is fortunate to reach its fifth birthday. In captivity, with food removed as a daily concern, wolves will live ten to 17 years, much like your dog. Starvation is the number one killer of wolves in the wild, and of mammals generally.

Other factors include attacks by other wolf packs, usually involving territory infringement and competition for prey, or being injured or killed by intended prey, as when wolves choose to attack an underestimated moose and get kicked in the skull or torso. Legal hunting and poaching by man are other major factors in many areas.

The starvation factor is most difficult for us to appreciate, as we live in a culture that provides safety nets, such as medical care, life insurance, unemployment, welfare, savings accounts, etc. In other words, whether I'm a great provider, or merely an adequate provider, I am protected against the strains of periods when I am less able to provide for my family.

While some predators, like foxes and goshawks may cache food, if you're a wolf or other predator, and you follow 8 months of successful hunting with several months of poor hunting, you and your family will likely starve. Any predator that so much as survives through a given year, is not only a good hunter, but probably a great hunter, or being supported by a great hunter.

A key factor in wolf survival is their jaws, which have 42 teeth, typically much larger teeth than dogs have, and set in a skull structure featuring powerful jaw muscles, which deliver a massive crushing power of 773 pounds psi at the carnassials, per Chrtiansen and Wroe, 2007. This is a serious bite. The jaws interlock, and with teeth specialized for tearing, gripping and power sufficient to crush bones, giving wolves access to more nutrition than would otherwise be available, serving as another hedge against starvation.

Cree and Zeebie 2011 by Terry Hawthorne, Soul Expression Photography.

Diseases like parvo virus and distemper take their toll, as do parasitic critters like the mite that causes mange. With respect to wolves from one pack killing trespassers from other packs, or transient wolves passing through a territory at the wrong place and time, alphas may kill three or four wolves from other packs during their lifetime.

Because of frequent turnover in the pack, there *are* times when an outsider of a given skill set, may enter the territory at the right time, becoming incorporated into the pack. Wolves also eliminate competition, by killing smaller predators, such as coyotes and foxes, when they encounter them, which enables a larger number of smaller prey animals for the wolves to take.

Wolves have scent glands on their tails, represented by a darker spot mid-tail, between the first two toes of their feet, and around their anus, glands which are used to leave an olfactory record of their traveling and rolling about.

Male and female urine have uniquely different odors, which indicate relative health, and in the case of females, whether they are in estrus. Defecation is also used as a scent marker.

Howling is just more wolf language. One howl says I'm here, where are you? A wolf who discovers a dead moose, or who kills a deer, may howl in place to alert other members of the pack, "I have something to show you", letting the sound of their howling and the scent of the dead prey lead pack members to the wolf. Other group howls may portray everything from pack contentment to mourning. Howling also identifies which wolf is howling, and whether they are a member of your pack.

For all these reasons, dispersing wolves must move quietly and carefully through neighboring wolf pack territories, lest they announce their presence, and are intercepted by rival pack members who probably won't welcome their presence.

Wolves, like dogs, wear their heart on their sleeves. Body posture, tail position and motion, hackles, and facial expressions, all indicate which wolf mood you are observing.

Wolf postures, Wikipedia, Public Domain.

Not only are dogs genetically gray wolves, but all dog behavior is basically modified wolf behavior. The principal difference between captive bred wolf behavior and dog behavior, as it pertains to interacting with humans, seems to be that dogs are more likely to obey orders from us, right down to following hand and eye signaling.

Ten to fifteen thousand years of being dogs has convinced dogs to not only heed the food and shelter provider, but to try to connect with us at an emotional, almost visceral level. Yes…. they appear to love us. I don't know what else to call it. Just as a mother and her nursing infant each experience a flow of oxytocin, the "happiness" drug within us all, so do you and your dog experience that nearly indescribable warm glow when you look at each other. It also appears that they can smell our emotions, which are accompanied by chemical changes in your body.

Captive bred wolves are just as affectionate physically. They'll lick your face and rough house with you, but on a personal level, they really don't appear to care what we think, and they're not interested in following pointing gestures, or whatever we're looking at.

Territory

Territoriality is a key factor in pack success. We should know, being nearly as territorial as wolves are. When I finished my tour of duty with the Marines in 1968, I moved to Manhattan to attend college, and had an apartment on the upper West Side. Naturally, I had neighbors living across the hall, and on either side of my apartment. Most were quiet and respectful. Others thought my music was insufferably loud.

Ten years later, my wife and I were in a modest house on about an acre of land in Westchester County, and our four children were starting to arrive. Part of the social contract demands consideration for your neighbors, so I promise not to go on your property, and cut down a

Christmas tree, while you're wintering in Florida, and so on. Now we live on 55 acres, and own the Adirondack Wildlife Refuge, but we still have neighbors north, south, east and west of us.

Lamar Valley wolf, Yellowstone, May 2018, by Steve Hall

A wolf packs territory is a community in which the wolves know most of the moose, and the moose all know most of the wolves. Like wolves, moose are mainly olfactory oriented, with each animal having its own identifying scent, in the same manner that your dog knows who you are as you have a uniquely identifying scent.

Let's say for sake of argument that a wolf pack in Alaska depends mainly on moose for their main source of nutrition. The pack needs to defend a territory large enough to ensure that there will be enough moose for the pack to make a living. Let's say the pack is having a great year, and there are enough moose, such that the pack is being careful, and choosing the right vulnerable moose for attack, and that the pack hasn't lost a single wolf to a moose, which are generally too dangerous to attack, when they're between two and ten years old.

Let's further say that a pack defending a territory north of our pack is having a lousy year. There aren't enough moose, and the wolves may become a little desperate, and find themselves attacking moose, which their better judgement might tell them to avoid, with the result that the pack has already lost two members to moose they had no business attacking.

Wolves may move about 20 to 50 miles per day, when they are looking for prey, and these wolves notice that when they are patrolling their territory, many of the moose they encounter are clustered near our pack's northern buffer zone, and they start making forays into our territory to poach some of our moose. If we catch their scent, or hear them howling back and forth, there will be fighting, wolves will be killed, packs reorganized and defended borders realigned.

Wolf packs defend territories ranging in size from 20

square miles to 2000 square miles, depending on the amount of prey of varying sizes available within their territory, the number of wolves in the pack, and the pressure of adjoining packs defending their territories.

Howling is an important means of communication among wolves, both within the pack, for example, to identify location viz a viz another pack member, or as a pack bonding activity, and between neighboring packs, as a means of avoiding confrontations by indicating a pack's current location. While the packs cover large territories, the boundaries of these territories are somewhat fluid, so, to avoid confrontations with neighboring packs, the pack may only enter the fringe buffer zone in pursuit of prey.

Alpha wolves continually mark their territories by "RLU", raised-leg urination, in males, and "FLU", flex-Leg urination in females, while submissive wolves, male or female, perform "SQUs", or urinations by squatting. Defecating is another form of marking, as is vigorously scratching the ground with the front paws, which opens the scent glands between their toes, thus leaving their scent as a warning to trespassers.

Our wolves get daily walks on the two miles of Wildlife Refuge trails before or after visitors have arrived for the day, an opportunity to get some exercise, while inspecting their "territory" for signs of prey or intruders, even though their main source of food are road-killed deer, freezer failures and deer carcasses cleaned by hunters. Cree growls when covering the scent spot of an unwelcome trespasser, like a black bear, coywolf or a local dog he does not like, while rolling on other scents.

Zeebie and Alex, by Terry Hawthorne, Soul Expression Photography.

While there is no definitive proof of why wolves and dogs roll in a scent, it may be a way of carrying information of some discovery back to the pack, so that the pack can decide whether to visit and perhaps appropriate the source of the odor. Perhaps it's an attempt at disguise, to confuse would be prey, or even a form of vanity, look what I found. We really don't know.

There are troubling examples of wolf packs in Yellowstone invading other packs territories for no other reason than to appear to want to kill other wolves, even if there does not seem to be any particular advantage in terms of having more prey at their disposal, as when the Mollies went after the famous wolf "06", as in "oh-six" and her Lamar Canyon pack, after attacking several other wolf packs defending territories in their general vicinity, as described in Nate Blakeslee's "American Wolf", a very fine book indeed.

As I said in the beginning, wolves are like us in ways we admire, and in ways we wish we were not!

Wolves, Algonquin Wolves and Coywolves

Based on computerized skull measurements, wolf taxonomist Ron Nowak distinguishes about 5 North American wolf subspecies, the Arctic, Mexican, Great Plains, Northwestern, and the Algonquin wolf, formally called the Eastern Wolf, examples of which can be seen in Algonquin Park, west of Ottawa.

Your average male wolf is about 90 pounds, with northern wolves slightly heavier, due to natural selection rewarding larger body mass, its heat retention capability, making larger wolves more likely to survive and reproduce, as described in "Bergman's Law", which covers mammals generally.

At the Adirondack Wildlife Refuge, Cree, a 14-year-old

wolf hybrid, of about 75% gray wolf ancestry, and a quarter Alaskan malamute weighs about 110 lbs., while eleven-year-old Zeebie, a full gray wolf and an example of a Great Plains wolf, is about 100 lbs. Kiska, a six year old female gray wolf is about 80 pounds.

Loyalty within the wolf pack is strong, and while you may observe much dominant posturing, snarling and growling by Cree, the gray male, born in 2006, in the role of older brother, and correspondingly submissive behavior by Zeebie, the younger blackish-turning-gray male, born in 2009, who resembles many of the wolves I see in Yellowstone, there is no actual violence. Look for Cree to carry himself upright, with his tail slightly cocked and raised in these encounters, and for Zeebie to approach Cree with a lowered posture, with tail down or tucked, while attempting to lick Cree's muzzle in a sign of deference. Our three wolves act like a pack, even though none of them are genetically related.

We are constantly asked whether we have wolves in the Adirondacks, to which the answer is occasionally, as in the wolf killed in 2021 by a hunter south of Cooperstown, one of about ten gray wolves killed by hunters in the Adirondacks the last twenty years, and whether we should reintroduce gray wolves to the Adirondack Park. The eastern coyote, variously called the coydog, coywolf, Adirondack wolf, or brush wolf, is genetically an Algonquin wolf-coyote hybrid, which explains why it tends to be sometimes twice the size of western coyotes.

Algonquin wolf, by Anne Fraser, Algonquin Provincial Park, Ontario.

There is a longitudinal west-east hybridization of gray wolves and western coyotes, originating in the Great Lakes region, with gray wolves leaning more to their gray wolf heritage but with perhaps 15% western coyote in their makeup. Gray wolves west of Minnesota are full gray wolves. The Algonquin wolf, protected and mainly based in the area of Algonquin Provincial Park, west of Ottawa, is a gray wolf hybridized with a western coyote, and about 60% gray wolf. There are wolf packs in

Algonquin Park which include Algonquin wolves and Coywolves.

So-called coydogs-coywolves of New England are a hybrid of coyotes and Algonquin wolves, which is why the coywolf has an average of 30% Algonquin wolf in them.

I believe when the Pilgrims landed on the Cape, when the English settled in Jamestown, in short, as Colonialists began populating the east coast, most of them were farmers and many had livestock. The Algonquin wolf probably ranged from Ontario and Quebec right down through the Carolinas.

In those days, when you saw a predator, such as a wolf or cougar, you shot it, and as settlers moved west through the Appalachians, they largely eliminated Algonquin wolves, leaving today's red wolf in the south and Algonquin wolves in Canada. The variation in DNA between the isolated red wolves and Algonquin wolves begin to drift, leaving the narrow differences between the two species today. The attempt to reintroduce red wolves to the Carolina coast is continually frustrated by the fact

A continent of canids

Opinions vary on wolf ranges and identities, but most researchers agree that the gray wolf once roamed across much of North America (including into Mexico, not shown) and that the coyote ranged across the west. A new genetic study finds that the red wolf and the eastern wolf (one from Quebec in Canada, bottom) arose later by mixing with coyotes as they expanded eastward.

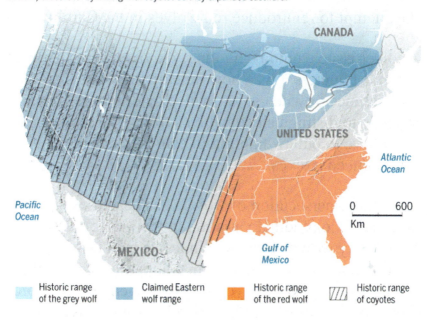

https://www.sciencemag.org/news/2016/07/how-do-you-save-wolf-s-not-really-wolf

that the red wolf readily mates with coyotes, and local hunters, unable to distinguish red wolves from coyotes, shoot them.

Something to ponder when considering the proposed reintroduction of wolves to the Adirondack Park: as of 2020, there are only an estimated 400 moose within the Park's 9,400 square miles, compared with 500 moose within Isle Royale's 200 square miles.

In addition, the wolves may eliminate many of the eastern coyote population within their territories, or perhaps more likely, water down the wolf genes by interbreeding with the coyotes, as has been happening in the attempt to reintroduce red wolves in the Carolinas.

Another issue would be hunting. I know from experience that most hunters, given how quickly they must react in the presence of wild canids, which tend to run, would struggle to distinguish coywolves from gray wolves, so we'd have to outlaw hunting of canids where you reintroduced wolves.

In fact, our persecution of wolves has helped exaggerate an existing logitudinal variation in wolf-coyote DNA. While gray wolves west of Minnesota tend to opportunistically kill coyotes in competition for smaller, safer prey, or to keep coyotes from scavenging wolf prey, there is evidence of interbreeding between wolves and coyotes from Minnesota east towards Ontario and Quebec.

Consider the following: young males disperse from their parents territory in the hopes of setting up and defending an unoccupied territory, for purposes of starting their own pack, or they hope to become the breeding male in an existing pack's territory. What if they don't encounter a female wolf who's willing to mate with them? They may end up mating with a female coyote or hybrid.

Dave Mech, of Isle Royale fame, author of some of my

favorite books on wolves, encouraged the Minnesota Science Center to experiment with interbreeding gray wolves and western coyotes, and while the results were a bit rocky, they did end up with some viable hybrid pups.

This sheds light on why Minnesota grays have about 15% coyote DNA, while the further east you go over Lake Superior into Ontario, Algonquin wolf country, the higher the DNA content rises, until you reach the Adirondacks and Maine, where so-called coydogs or coywolves have up to thirty percent Algonquin wolves in their makeup.

Cree and Zeebie, by Aleah Leighton

More information on wolf reintroduction from a ten year old study is available at "wolf-reintroduction-feasibility-in-the-adirondacks". As crazy about wolves as we are, Northern Maine may prove to be a better candidate for supporting the reintroduction of wolves.

Why are we where we are today? In the nineteenth and early twentieth centuries, mainly on behalf of hunting and ranching lobbies, but also because individual citizens routinely shot predators, our persecution of wolves steadily decimated wolf numbers until the mid-teens to early nineteen twenties, when the feds got involved, and we carried out federal poisoning campaigns, which sounded the death knell for wolves everywhere in the lower forty eight, except in Minnesota where the good citizens kept the feds out.

Some naturalists had already figured out that wolves were critical precisely because they kept deer and coyote numbers in check and warned that deer and coyote explosions would follow the extermination of wolves, but their warnings went unheeded. For example, Aldo Leopold said, "While a buck pulled down by wolves can be replaced in two or three years, a range pulled down by too many deer may fail of replacement in as many decades," a statement which rings true everywhere Americans have experienced the huge increase in deer numbers.

With wolves out of the way, western coyotes began their

manifest destiny in reverse, mainly heading east under the Great Lakes, looking to set up new territories so successfully, that by the seventies and eighties, folks who grew up anywhere from the midwest to east coast began seeing western coyotes, even though they hadn't seen them as kids.

Coyotes don't have passports, and don't know where international boundaries lie, so many of them went northwest over Lake Superior, where they ran into a Canadian wolf called the eastern wolf, recently renamed the Algonquin wolf. Just as gray wolves and western coyotes had split into their individual species between a million and two million years ago, so had the Algonquin wolf split off from the coyote- wolf line about 150,000 years ago. These are hardly settled guesses but bear with me.

In other words, when western coyotes began flooding back into Canada, they were running into a smaller wolf, which, like the gray wolf, might kill them to prevent competition for a larger base of safer, smaller prey. It was a smaller wolf, because it was a gray wolf – coyote hybrid, containing about 20% coyote. To complicate matters, a young male Algonquin wolf, who may have been unsuccessful in encountering a female Algonquin wolf to share his new territory, mated with a western coyote. Apparently there was a new wave of such mating

Adirondack Coywolf, packmate eyes in rear, trail cam at Adirondack Wildlife Refuge, by Steve Hall.

Every habitat has what we call a carrying capacity, whether you're talking about plants, trees, bugs etc.... or, in this case, mammals. If there are too many wolves, and not quite enough territory, prospective mates or prey, something has to give, which it did, and we saw an influx of these further hybridized coywolves into the Adirondack Mountains, from which they've been gradually spreading out in all directions, such that, as a kid, I never saw a coyote in the Adirondacks back in the fifties and sixties, whereas today we have an enduring healthy pack, which considers the Wildlife Refuge part of its territory.

Cree and Zeebie, by Terry Hawthorne, Soul Expression Photography.

It also means that these coywolves, which locals call "coydogs", which they most decidedly are not, are running into western coyotes, pushing in from the west, under the Great Lakes, so we see coyotes who are the same size as the western coyotes in Yellowstone, about thirty to forty pounds, but also these coywolves, which range for forty to sixty pounds, with an average Algonquin wolf share of about thirty per cent.

One personal experience I don't understand, is that when I'm out on the Refuge hiking trails with Cree alone, we have twice run into a coywolf, who I have run into on my own several times, in which case the coywolf simply runs away. When I was with Cree, this same coywolf responded with abject terror, seeming to freeze in place for about ten seconds, his body posture expressing this fear, while Cree's reaction is more curiosity or "whatever" than anything else. Perhaps it's because Cree is on a long chain and doesn't wish me to go horizontal on him!

Isle Royale Study

Isle Royale is a 200 square mile island in Lake Superior, about 15 miles from the international shore-line boundary where Minnesota meets Ontario. Moose swam to Isle Royale about 100 years ago, and wolves wandered across the ice from the mainland about 50 years later, during a bitterly cold Winter.

Warming climate has made it unlikely that more wolves will be crossing over any time soon, so Isle Royale sits out in Superior as a perfect natural laboratory, enabling the longest continuous study of predator-prey relationships in the history of modern science.

On Isle Royale, the principal prey of the wolf are moose, and over the fifty years of the study, the number of resident moose on the island, has ranged been the 500 surveyed in 2009, to a high of 2,500 in 1998, while the number of wolves varied from a dozen to 50, with average being about 20 wolves spread over 2 or 3 packs. In 2010, there were 19 wolves comprising 2 packs, whereas in 2009, there were 22 wolves in 5 packs, in addition to a couple of loners who lead furtive lives, scavenging at the edges of territories. In 2010, there was estimated to be 510 moose.

Cape Breton bull moose, Sept 2017, by Steve Hall.

The great majority of wolves on Isle Royal can trace their ancestry to an original female, which has caused severe inbreeding among the Isle Royale wolves. By 2018, there were only two wolves left on Isle Royale, so four Canadian wolves were captured and dropped on the island in March of 2019, as a first step in reviving and continuing the wolf-moose study. You may follow the annual reports and articles from Isle Royale at www.isleroyalewolf.org.

While wolf predation is an important contributing factor,

particularly when moose numbers are down and wolf numbers are up, moose are also affected by over-browsing of balsam fir, hot summers, deep winter snow, which affects the ability of moose to move around more so than it affects wolves, the amount of infestation by winter ticks, as well as the mite that causes mammalian mange.

Another serious problem for an animal that in maturity consumes an average of five tons of vegetation per year. is the gradual deterioration and breakdown of tooth and jaw. While virtually all older moose sooner or later develop arthritis, a recent important study by Peterson found a correlation between earlier onset of arthritic joints in moose born to undernourished cows. The average lifespan of moose on Isle Royale is 12 years for bulls and 16 for cows, with 20 being the record.

Wolves are affected by starvation, mange, distemper, and introduced diseases like parvo.

The wolves tend to take mainly older, arthritic or otherwise infirm moose, as well as bulls weakened by exhaustion and the injuries they may sustain during the autumn rut. Calves are another important target, but in 2009, no adolescents were taken during the winter, there being an abundance of older moose. Once moose reach the age of two, and particularly when they reach the breeding age of five, and until they are nine or ten, they are less vulnerable to wolf attack.

A mature moose in the prime of life weighs anywhere from 700 to 1,500 pounds, and is quite capable of defending itself with kicks to the head, torso and legs of a wolf, and, in the case of bulls between May and November, swings of those enormous antlers, which can weigh 50 pounds, so the pack is wary of attacking such an animal, and may test the same moose many times over a period of years, before deciding the moose is one day vulnerable enough to risk an attack.

The correlation between the numbers of wolves and moose can have a generationally delayed affect. For example, if over browsing leads to malnutrition in moose calves, which live shorter lives because of earlier onset of arthritis, this will initially provide wolves with greater numbers of older, potential prey animals. In turn, the wolf pups, less apt to starve, survive and breed, but their offspring are then subject to fewer older moose to prey on, causing wolf numbers to crash.

In nature, all events, processes and players are connected. Wolves are "apex predators", meaning top of the food chain predators, in much the same way as are loons, fishers and the Eastern Coyote in the Adirondacks. Wolves are also "keystone" predators, meaning that their impact in each habitat, will have ramifications far beyond the animals they prey on.

Wolves also go after their competition, coyotes, as a way

of ensuring a larger base of smaller, safer prey, such as deer, snowshoe hare and beaver, just as coyotes go after red fox to sustain a larger base of rodents. Wolf presence in habitat also carries benefits for creatures not normally associated with wolves. For example, who suspected that the reintroduction of wolves into Yellowstone National Park would improve the survivability of trout?

Cree howls to Zeebie and, with Steve in the Wolf Meadow, waits for response, by Adirondack Wildlife Refuge.

Before wolves were reintroduced, elk tended to congregate around the streams, lakes and rivers in Yellowstone, over browsing cottonwoods and willows, while trampling other streamside vegetation, causing erosion, thus making creeks broader and shallower, cutting down the shade which helps keep water at the cooler temperatures trout prefer.

Because of wolves reducing elk numbers, and teaching

them to avoid hanging around water ways, stream and river side vegetation has somewhat recovered, helping the trout, but also, with willows, cottonwoods and understory shrubbery being left to mature, providing nesting sites for songbirds, and food, along with den and dam building materials, for beaver, whose numbers increased, *even though they are occasionally taken by wolves.*

Even pronghorn antelope were helped by the return of wolves to Yellowstone. While mature pronghorns are way too fast for predators, cougars and coyotes both prey on pronghorn calves, with the latter adept at locating young pronghorns. While an individual cougar can handle an individual wolf, the fact that cougars may run into groups of wolves makes them reluctant to come down out of the hill country and get caught out in the open. And while wolves may eliminate a third of the coyotes within their territories but have so far not yet focused on pronghorn calves as coyotes do, pronghorns have increased since the wolf's reintroduction.

Cree and Zeebie discussing politics, with Alex looking on, by Terry Hawthorne, Soul Expression Photography.

2 WOLVES, HUMANS & DOGS

We've had several hiking dogs, but two of my favorites were Chino, a wolf-husky mix we brought back from Alaska in 1990, and Roscoe, a nondescript gene pool who looked like a million other mutts you've seen, and whose ancestry is anyone's guess. Our oldest son, Dan, another animal lover, became a veterinarian and later a veterinary cardiologist, partly because of his experiences with Chino. He also does some pro-bono care, which led to our adopting Roscoe as a pup around 2005.

Both canids had a long history of High Peaks hiking with us. Chino hiked his last peak, Dix, in 2002, and died in 2004, a year before Roscoe came on the scene, and continued the hiking tradition. The other common thread between them? Porcupines!

Most Adirondack dog owners have porcupine stories. We were fortunate in that our stories were all local, not out on the trail, deep in the High Peaks, miles from the car, and any assistance.

Roscoe with Steve on Macomb Mountain in the Dix Range Wilderness, by Steve.

When Chino was ten, he was so badly quilled on our property, the Adirondack Wildlife Refuge, that he resembled those grainy old photographs of the heavily bearded Tolstoy. Thereafter, when Chino would accompany me on morning jogs along the Wolf Walk Trail at the Refuge, if we encountered a porcupine ambling across the forest floor from one tree trunk to another, Chino would get excited, start to charge, and then he'd stop in his tracks, and look back at me, as if to say, "oh yeah, I remember how this turns out!" He was never quilled again.

Roscoe, on the other hand, has been quilled about ten times. Someone alert Guinness. One vet, who has an interest in canine psychology, explained that Roscoe had an inner rage against his prickly neighbors, and really couldn't help himself. Mmm.... Anyone who knew Roscoe would suggest that the words "Roscoe" and "rage" don't belong in the same sentence.

Chino by Steve Hall

While most rural dogs suffer one or two painful lessons in porcupine avoidance, it struck me that here were two

canids, Chino and Roscoe, each with a friendly and unassuming personality, both facing porcupines in the exact same environment, with such different results. Of course, two samples hardly constitute a study, but the fact that Chino was mostly gray wolf, encouraged me to wonder again, why do wolves appear to be smarter than dogs, and what does "smarter" in this context mean?

Socialized wolves can be just as affectionate as dogs, but while they may treat you like a trusted member of the pack, they are more rooted in their own interests and activities, less dependent on you, and less likely to automatically accompany you, when you walk from one place to another. They're also generally less responsive to our cues. Dogs have been shown to be more responsive to human signs and signals than even chimps or bonobos, our nearest relatives on earth.

Where wolves excel is in learning from each other, and in working things out. There was an interesting experiment at an Austrian Wolf Science Center, in which several dogs and socialized wolves were led into an enclosure with their handlers, one team at a time. The enclosure contained a small wooden crate, with a treat inside, sort of a canine rubik's cube. Each wolf and dog observed a pre-trained dog locate the latch, open the box and retrieve the treat. Individual dogs and wolves were then given the opportunity to try to retrieve the treat in similar fashion.

None of the dogs could repeat what they had seen done by the trained dog. They would eventually give up, and look back at the master, the food provider, the companion who is always there to ultimately solve any problems they encounter. Dogs, it appeared, were better at learning from their human companions, than from other dogs. All the wolves retrieved the treat on the first try, and none of them ever looked back at their handlers. Why would you be any better at this than I am?

How Did Dogs Happen?

If dogs are indeed "man's best friend", how did that happen? From an evolutionary perspective, where do dogs come from? Are modern dogs the result of domestication of wolves by Cro-Magnon or Anatomically Modern Humans? Is it that simple?

Genetics often provides definitive answers to individual questions, solid evidential milestones, which demand explanation from other sciences working with sketchier, less cohesive clues. Mitochondrial DNA studies by Robert K. Wayne of UCLA indicated that those wolves which eventually led to dogs began veering away from their wild brethren over 135,000 years ago. This was about 60,000 years before our ancestors left Africa. Could those wolves be the ancestors of both modern gray wolves as well as dogs?

At the same time, paleontologists point to the oldest dog remains found to date, which are only about 15,000 years old (Russia) or 30,000 years old (Belgium), depending on which site's findings you agree with. They're "dogs" in the sense that their skeletal features are arguably not wolves.

Zeebie and Kiska at the Adirondack Wildlife Refuge, by Joe Kostoss, Eye in the Park.

About the only thing canid experts agree on today, is that domestic dogs, regardless of breed, are genetically wolves. That's where the fun starts. How, when and where some wolves began adapting their behavior, on their way to becoming "dogs", the first domesticated animal, is still a matter of considerable dispute. And how long did it take for the gradual change in physical attributes to become evident?

Wolves, Humans, Dogs & Civilization

Over the past twenty years, the speculation has drifted towards the idea that some wolves domesticated themselves after humans began trading their hunter-gatherer lifestyle for settlement life, making human settlements along rivers and animal migration routes from about 40,000 to 10,000 years ago, and started husbandry and agriculture about 15,000 years ago.

As Raymond Coppinger suggested in "Dogs", some wolves found they could make an easier living hanging around the village scrap heap, and some of these, perhaps omega wolves or lone wolves, those who had more difficult lives making a living out in the wild, developed shorter flight distances from approaching humans, and these were the animals who began breeding around the outskirts of the villages, and depended directly on the waste generated by the village, as well as the deer, rodents and other scavengers drawn by agriculture and husbandry.

While these wolves were hardly pets, they did serve as warning systems for scavenging predators, as well as approaching humans, so an uneasy alliance was born. However, with the newer Mitochondrial evidence, it's time for some serious speculating about the pre-settlement relationships with wolves.

Your ancestors left Africa about 70,000 years ago. Aside from the number of related homo ancestors, our nearest living genetic ancestor is a type of chimpanzee. When making that claim in America, one better add "whether we like it or not", as many Americans tend to deny scientific evidence.

Homo erectus learned to control fire about a million years ago, which not only kept our ancestors warm, allowing Neanderthals and anatomically modern humans (Homo Sapiens) to move into colder climates, but it also led to cooking meat to make it easier for our jaws, with an average crushing power of 250 pounds per square inch, to process and consume, while incidentally killing dangerous pathogens.

Campfires led to more socializing and communication in clans, staying up after dark, more exchange of ideas, discouraging the approach of predators, while directed burns allowed us to move potential prey into killing zones or killed potential prey animals outright.

During the agricultural revolution, modern humans gradually transitioned from nomadic hunter gatherers to farmers, which led to the first housing boom, as folks staying in one place, and tied to the land, wanted to at least get out of the weather. Building rudimentary shelters, and no longer being completely at the mercy of the seasons, changed life dramatically for human beings. Even our wolf dogs were greatly affected, changing the mating cycles of bitches, who became able to mate two to four times a year.

The Pleistocene Stage

The partnership of man and dog was playing out during the last 100,000 years of the two million year Pleistocene, during which astronomical climate factors like the Milankovic cycles, working with individual climate events like the aftermath of the Mount Toba eruption, caused plummeting global temperatures, and the surging and retreating of ice sheets.

Typical Mammoth Steppe scene, from Wikipedia, Public Domain.

Swollen by evaporating and precipitating ocean waters, glaciers spread out from higher elevations and north facing ravines and valleys, across northern latitudes, while ocean levels dropped, as much as 350 feet during the glacial maximum. Much of the northern landscape was rendered uninhabitable for vegetation, wildlife and earlier peoples such as Neanderthals in Europe and Homo Erectus across Asia, sometimes driving them south into conflicts with our ancestors, many of whom who were moving north and west out of Africa. The receding ocean waters exposed land bridges like Berengia between Siberia and Alaska, where the Bering Sea drained, allowing, where ice-free valleys and coasts remained, the gradual migration, of plant and animal species back and forth between continents.

These periods would be followed by periods of warming called interglacials, during which the melting glaciers would not only cause rising seas, which closed off continental bridges, but opened up more of the northern areas to a resurgence of life, where the Mammoth Steppe ranged from present day Spain to Alaska. The tundra-like Steppe was a relatively treeless biome, characterized by grasslands, low shrubs, mosses and lichens, and the mammoths and wooly rhinos that thrived there, along with herding ungulates like horse, reindeer, bison and the ancestor of today's domestic cattle, aurochs.

The People

Mitochondrial and Y chromosome DNA place our ancestors in East Africa around 160,000 years ago. Further evidence suggests that a group of about 150 people, the ancestors of the modern human race, homo sapiens, migrated out of Africa through the Gates of Grief across the mouth of the Red Sea, about 90,000 years ago, and over the next 15,000 years or so, gradually expanded along the seacoasts of India and southeast Asia.

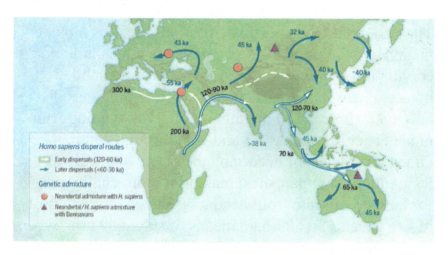

Homo sapiens dispersal routes out of Africa, Wikipedia.

While this certainly was not the first exodus out of Africa, it was the only one that has endured until anatomically modern humans came north into Europe around the western Mediterranean about 55,000 years ago. The Mount Toba eruption on Sumatra around 75,000 years ago, buried much of the Indian sub-continent under 15 feet of ash, causing a nuclear winter and instant mini-ice age, which reduced the early human population to about 10,000.

Homo Erectus ranged from 2 million to 300,000 years ago, and it is believed they started losing their thick body hair around 1.2 million years ago. Neanderthal history stretches from about 400,000 to 40,000 years ago, and like homo sapiens they were relatively hairless, compared to primate relatives.

The various reasons postulated for hairlessness include the hyper development of sweat glands which aid in cooling through the evaporation of sweat, which left homo sapiens, a not particularly swift mammal, as the only one who can run marathons. Wolves and dogs run much faster, but not as far and cool through panting. Other advantages of becoming the naked ape were the lessening of skin parasites, making it more challenging for them to migrate from head to groin, etc. The control of fire gave us an alternate means of staying warm, when not burning energy running about, and the donning of furs and skins of other animals helped both Neanderthals and Modern Humans stay warm as they moved into more northerly, colder climates.

As homo sapiens moved north and northwest out of Africa, our skin color began to lighten, as it was not subjected to the high levels of ultraviolet light our ancestors were in Africa. This is why the farther north our ancestors wandered, the lighter our skin became.

While the glaciers began to recede in Europe and Asia over the next 50,000 years, ancestral expansion along the coasts of Southeast Asia and Japan, as well as inland towards southern Europe, Central Asia and Siberia, brought nomadic peoples closer to Beringia. North America remained under an enormous mile thick sheet extending as far south as the Great Lakes and the Adirondacks, but a corridor from Alaska down to the US and Canadian border area, allowed the first ancestors of Native Americans to cross the Bering Land Bridge into Alaska, and down across to the areas of the Great Lakes.

The glacial maximum of about 15 – 20 thousand years ago, sealed up Alaska again, until the last interglacial, which we are essentially still living in, opened up North America, and allowed the ancestors of Native Americans to spread up into central and eastern Canada, and down through Central and South America.

Paleoclimatologists like Curt Stager of Paul Smiths, refer to our period as the Anthropocene, as mankind is the first keystone species on earth, whose activities are directly affecting climate. The natural forces which drive climate change include solar cycles, earthquakes, volcanoes, and plate tectonic mega-disasters like the Deccan Plates, the occasional and sometimes devastating asteroid impact, the tilt and wandering of the earth's axis, eccentricity of earth's orbit, not to mention plant and animal respiration.

We're adding anthropogenically elevated CO_2 and methane levels, resulting in rising sea levels and ocean acidification, to mention just two dangerous aspects, leading us into uncharted futures, starting with the possible interruption of the next ice age, which may sound appealing after a rough winter, but may also carry with it other, less desirable features.

The Dogs

Canidae, the family of wolves, coyote, wild dogs, foxes and jackals, evolved in North America starting about 10 million years ago, when a gradual shifting of terrain from forest to grasslands, and the abundance of food thus provided, enabled the development of larger grazers and browsers, such as camels, horses, and caribou.

Camels and horses first evolved in what became Western America and went extinct there after their descendants crossed Beringia into Asia. Caribou originated in northwestern America and southwestern Canada. Reindeer in Russia and Scandinavia are domesticated caribou. The predators of these ungulates became larger over time, as only the larger canids could successfully hunt them, and therefore live to breed, and pass along the genes for larger canids.

The ancestors of wolves, not to mention many other large mammals, crossed one of the many iterations of Berengia and the Bering Land Bridge into Asia and Europe and back multiple times. The ancestral wolves kept increasing in size, honing the hunting skills that turned them into the first mammalian pastoralists, that is, predators who survived by following the great herds of caribou, horses and bison, which traversed the mammoth steppe and the American Plains, and using cooperative hunting tactics within the pack, to pick off and remove the very young, the very old, the sick and lame, in short, the animals who were not fast enough or strong enough to defend themselves from attacks by wolves.

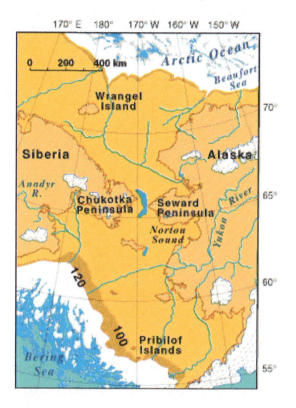

Beringia, from Wiki Commons, Public Domain.

Since wolves, in the interests of self-preservation, avoid attacking the strongest and fittest, their culling activities tend to strengthen the herds by removing the animals which you don't want breeding anyway. When you think about it, wolves were apparently "herding" free ranging ungulates long before we existed.

Able to retreat to the warmth of our homes, with our food and water on demand, we may experience nature as this beautiful and balanced creation, but if you're an animal trying to make a living out there, it's not a democracy, and fairness isn't a factor.

Love 'em or hate 'em, predators have arguably the most dangerous job in the animal kingdom, as there's nothing more dangerous than attacking other animals, particularly, as in the case of wolves, when those intended prey animals are often anywhere from two to twenty times the wolf's size.

This is why, for example, wolf packs in North America, will test, on average about twenty moose, for each one they deem sufficiently vulnerable to risk an all-out attack. It also explains why moose between the ages of two and ten, who remain healthy, have little to fear from wolf attack, and have much greater problems than the fact that many of them live among wolves. Contrary to opinions nourished by movies and popular media, most predators would much rather locate a food source which is already dead, and therefore not defensively dangerous to the attacking predator who wishes to harvest its protein.

Wolves lead short and dangerous lives. They can be killed by other wolves during territory disputes, or by choosing the wrong bison or moose as prey. They can be shot or trapped, legally and illegally by people, or poisoned, and then there's always starvation, which tends to be the number one killer of most wildlife. The average life span of a wolf is about 5 years in the wild. In Yellowstone, the competition is so severe that only one out of five wolves reaches their second birthday. Raised in captivity, fed regularly, like your dog, wolves live ten to fifteen years.

Into a World Fraught with Peril

As our African ancestors came out of the trees and onto the spreading savannahs, they were shifting from a largely frugivorous diet to the omnivorous diets of hunter-gatherers. A cooling climate favored wild grasses and tundra vegetation over fruit bearing trees and plants, and expanding glaciers in the north, and the dry, cold winds they enable, caused deserts in the south. The first failed exit of homo sapiens from Africa was to the Levant about 125,000 years ago, through a green and vibrant area that became the Sahara Desert. It is possible that those early people ran into bands of Neanderthals retreating south because of encroaching glaciers. Whether it was the desertification of the area, or the Neanderthal competition, or elements of both, our first foray out of Africa was literally a dead end.

We needed the protein you get from meat, and that meant scavenging and hunting. Homo erectus had begun cooking meat 780,000 years before, and the group's campfires also provided warmth and protection against some of the most dangerous predators that ever lived.

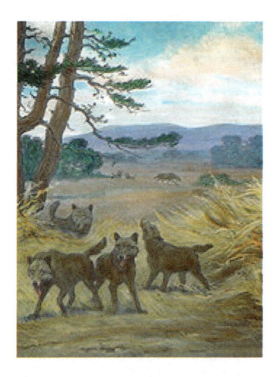

Restoration of a dire wolf pack in Rancho La Brea by Charles R. Knight, 1922, Wikipedia, Public Domain.

At the top of the food chain were six types of saber toothed cats, half of them larger than today's Amur tiger, the largest, most dangerous and most endangered cat in the world today. There were short-faced bears twice the size of grizzlies, and unlike today's omnivorous black and brown bears, these bears, judging from their dentition, were strict carnivores. They were not pigeon-toed like todays bears and were so fast they could run down fleeing prey.

There was a larger wolf called the dire wolf, the most common mammalian fossil unearthed at the famous La Brea tar pits, and now a media star in the "Game of Thrones". New research suggests that Dire Wolves are not really canids related to gray wolves. There were cave lions, cave hyenas, and the huge vegan cave bear. It was not a safe time to wander away from the campfire.

La Brea Tar Pits, from Wikpedia, Public Domain.

Spears and flint knives were probably useless in the face of such predators. Imagine growing up in an environment, knowing that if you met one of these predators away from the campfire, and they were hungry, your life ended. And if you had forayed out by yourself, your family members would never find out what had become of you.

With respect to early hunting weapons, projectile points 500,000 years old were found in Africa, and the oldest preserved spears found are from 400,000 years ago in Germany, probably used by early Neanderthals. Generally, wooden spears and arrow shafts don't preserve well, but it is postulated that the main Neanderthal hunting weapons were throwing and thrusting spears with stone and flint projectile points, rock throwing slings and stone hammers.

Anatomically modern humans lived in Neanderthal occupied areas from 45 to 40,000 years ago, with Neanderthals disappearing about 40,000 years ago. Many argue that the superiority of Sapiens hunting weapons left Neanderthals unable to compete, but most of these weapons, such as atlatls (spear throwers), bow and arrows, didn't appear until Neanderthals were already gone. New theories suggest homo sapiens lived in larger groups, and Neanderthal groups were not only smaller but more far apart, and so suffered from less experiential knowledge transfers than our ancestors benefited from.

Yellowstone grizzly sow with cubs, 2016 by Steve Hall.

Eating meat off the bone and dropping the remains ten feet from where you planned to sleep that night, was not a very sound tactic, because the very predators we feared were principally attracted by the smell of meat. When you fire up the grill in Yellowstone, every grizzly within 4 miles down wind of your camp site, knows what you're cooking, and fortunately for you, would prefer not to meet you. When the short faced bear showed up, lured by the wonderful smells around our ancestors' camp fire, he found himself in two frames of mind: on the one hand, he was afraid of the fire, but on the other, he was overwhelmed by the desire to harvest the source of those delectable odors.

Our ancestors probably learned from painful experience that a much better plan, was to set up a bone pile, a scrap heap, maybe 100 yards from the main campfire, and out in the open, to act as a filter, drawing whatever scavenging-minded predators were in the area. Since our still evolving frugivore teeth were not very efficient at stripping meat off bones, we left a scavenger's treasure trove of good food at the bone pile. This would act as a rather valuable census, and answer basic questions like, is it safe to gather some firewood, not to mention make deliveries to the bone pile. It was also an excellent olfactory way to hang a "Free Lunch!" sign, to keep drawing the predators after the group had moved on.

With the bone pile in place, the bears and big cats would probably be drawn to the scrap heap, where they might encounter either lone wolves, or a pack of wolves, who proceeded to defend their food source. Predators engage in a tremendous amount of bluffing and threatening. The strategy is to persuade your competitor to leave the food source. Actual physical contact is a last resort, because if you must resort to fighting, that's when you get hurt.

From time to time, visitors to the Wildlife Refuge will witness our wolves in toothsome and growly dispute. We sometimes must point out that there is no blood, and what they're witnessing is the equivalence of a shoving match over a deer leg, or a favorite spot to stretch out, a dispute that dissipates as quickly as it began, but can sound rather aggressive.

The point is, since there were more wolves than bears or cats, and since the wolves, just as today, were probably afraid of us, the hairless ape who screams, and hurls rocks and spears, our ancestors began to look at the wolves, as an early warning system. The wolves, in turn, saw us as a possible provider of food, and an adversary who was safe to be around, if you didn't approach too closely.

Kiska as a pup, by Terry Hawthorne, Soul Expression Photography.

It is also likely that our ancestral hunters would occasionally come across abandoned or orphaned wolf pups from time to time. Wolf pups are not only quite adorable, but quite manageable, if they're imprinted on people at less than a month old. Wolves may have become not only the first pets and beasts of burden, but also an animal who could warm the sleeping furs, as well as a form of property, which could be exchanged in trade, and, in times of severe hunger, something that could be eaten.

Hunter-Gatherers on the Mammoth Steppe

Our nomadic ancestors probably discovered that following the bison, horse and reindeer herds on the Mammoth Steppe, offered the best opportunities for obtaining meat, so they began mimicking the pastoral wolves, getting the ungulates used to having humans around, who would pick off the very weak, old, lame, young and, better still, dead ungulates. They also discovered that they could combine rock throwing, screaming, mobbing, and just generally intimidating behavior, as a means of driving wolves and even occasionally larger predators off *their* kills.

However, consider how dangerous hunting was in those days. Picture modern horses, which appear in the fossil record about 5 million years ago, or roughly 25 times as far back as we go. Large animals, ranging from 700 to 1,200 pounds. Domesticating and riding horses only started about 4,000 years ago, so for well over ninety-five percent of our history with horses, we were trying to hunt and kill them for meat, using crude spears and much later arrows. If you've ever wondered why hunters are so revered in prehistory, it's because they had suicidal jobs.

Naturalistic reconstruction of Ötzi, who died in the French Alps, frozen in a glacier, 5,300 years ago, By Theodoros Karasavvas,- South Tyrol Museum of Archaeology. Source: Public Domain

Our ancestors probably preferred strategic hunting, trying to stampede horses or bison off a cliff, or into a canyon, perhaps using torches and movable physical barriers to trap them inside. The former method might provide more meat for us, than we could drag away, so we'd end up feeding the other predators and scavengers. The latter would allow us to hurl large stones and spears from a safer distance above the panicked animals. Either way, it's hard to imagine the wolves hearing, seeing or smelling the carnage, and not racing to take advantage.

Grizzly bears sometimes head in the direction of a gun shot during elk season. Similarly, as wolves began to realize that our ancestors were quite clever at setting up ambushes and providing meat, it's easy to imagine them following us when we appeared with weapons, or depending on circumstance, even us following them, since they were much better at locating the herds than we were.

If wolves approached the same horses we were stalking, and they observed us wounding an animal already under pressure from the wolves, it would make sense that the opportunistic wolves would immediately attack the injured animal, with the result that the terribly hazardous activity of hunting started to become somewhat safer for our ancestors. Our wounded prey, who may have wanted to flee, or even attack us, would have to contend with harassing wolves.

Slowly, over thousands of years of such behavior, an uneasy alliance of convenience was born. The wolves began to realize that our ability to figure out how to use the terrain to kill many of the large ungulates in one place, meant they might eat more consistently, and have a better shot at survival, than if they continued to patrol and defend their territories. Many of the wolves took up permanent residence at the bone pile, and routinely followed our hunters on their daytime hunts. Even today, hunters accompanied by dogs consistently bring home more game than hunters who don't.

Bolder wolves might position themselves at a safe distance away from the campfire at night, their eyes reflecting the fire light, and their vigilance, their interest in protecting themselves and other pack members, made them perfect inadvertent watch dogs for our ancestors. While wolves bark infrequently, and not in annoying clusters the way dogs do, when they bark, it's generally to alert other wolves, or to get the attention of another predator, as when they may try to drive a bear off a carcass. Wolves, like bears, also emit a low "wuff" sound, generally when they're surprised at discovering a person or other animal too close to them.

The point is that our ancestors would come to understand these signals after long exposure to them, and the further they were from the safety of the fire, the more critical such information would be. From the wolves' point of view, our bone piles may have served as what we call rendezvous sites today. From the peoples' point of view, they would begin to recognize individual wolves, and while most wolves would be careful about approaching people, some wolves learned to exploit their relationship with the people of the clan.

Aside from socializing, telling stories, and working on weapons and honing flint, there wasn't a whole lot to do around the campfire at night.

José María Velasco (1840 - 1912) – Scene from the Quaternary upper Paleolithic Period, Public Domain

Consider the following: Writing is only about 5,000 years old, having been first developed by the Sumerians in

Mesopotamia, the cradle of civilization and site of modern-day Iraq and Syria. Writing, such as cuneiform, became critical as mid-eastern economies, with the development of two wheeled horse drawn carts, and the proliferation of beasts of burden like camels, depended on trade and moving goods around, what quantities of x are being transported to y, etc. Writing was preceded by something called the oral tradition, which developed when language itself first developed.

Language, the distillation of sounds from human calls and gestures, through Phonemes, the basic units of human sound, probably started before our ancestors left Africa, and was probably critical to the whole migration process. African "click" languages of the Khoisan language families contain 100 phonemes, but as language evolved through thousands of years, the further you got from original migration routes, the more languages contain a lower number of phenomes. Why does any of this matter?

To understand the oral tradition in crude terms, think of the last time you repeated a joke you'd heard. Did you alter the joke, improve it, or did it fall flat? As the joke gets passed around, it changes, as everyone telling the joke puts their own spin on it. When our ancestors were sitting around the campfire at night, clan elders would probably provide both entertainment and education, by standing up and repeating the stories they'd learned as young people in the same clan. These stories included both educational information, and often a moral, including practical advice on what works and what doesn't.

Anthropologists tell us that large clans might contain as many as 200 people, manageable enough that individuals could be expected to give up individual urges and desires, often inimical to group interests.

What was it like sitting around the campfire? As you looked across the flames, you probably saw the eyes of relatives, and if the clan was large enough, the eyes of relative strangers. Looking beyond them, you saw a second ring of eyes, the wolves, who had learned they could make an adequate living at the bone pile, and a better living around the campfire. Perhaps the first wolves who hung around our ancestors were omegas, wolves who found it easier to make a living around human beings than they would in their natal pack.

From the kid's point of view, think of these campfire lectures as early education. As any teacher will tell you, kids learn at different rates, which means the kids around the campfire would hear many of these stories again and again, with some kids bored by the repetition, as others were still struggling to understand. The development of religions shared many of these stories, which explains why many western religions contain similar stories, such as the Noah story. Many of the stories that ended up in the Old Testament, about 3,500 years old, as well as the texts of other modern religions, are older than the religions themselves.

Bored family members might amuse themselves by occasionally tossing meat fragments and bones to the wolves, further cementing the uneasy bond between them.

Going out on a limb!

The key to the divergence between wolves and the ancestors of dogs may have to do with breeding pools. In other words, wolves who hung around nomadic ancestral clans, tended more and more to breed amongst their own, and less and less with wild wolves. Did this eventually turn them into a different species? No, because one of the ways of differentiating species, is determining whether they can breed. Some canids can interbreed, and wolves and dogs are the same species. Wolves are canis lupus, while dogs are canis lupus familiaris. We have had two wolf hybrids, Chino being the first. If you've met Cree at the Wildlife Refuge, he is three quarters wolf, and one quarter malamute, while Zeebie is a full Great Plains Wolf.

Wolves can also interbreed with coyotes. While gray wolves tend to kill western coyotes, as they represent competition for food, experiments by renowned wolf researcher L. David Mech and the Minnesota Science Center, demonstrated that gray wolves can produce offspring with western coyotes. Furthermore, Eastern wolves, such as those found in Algonquin Park, and sibnce renamed Algonquin wolves, are already part coyote, going back long before the arrival of man, and they do interbreed with western coyotes passing above the great lakes, producing the Eastern coyote, or coywolf, which we have in the Adirondacks.

There is, of course, no direct evidence that wolves participated even indirectly in hunting with ancestral humans, but there are two findings and one recent theory that need reconciling. The first fact is the Mitochondrial evidence mentioned earlier, the fact that the DNA of the wolves which probably became the ancestors of dogs, began to veer away from wolf DNA about 135,000 years ago.

The more we learn about Neanderthals, their build and strength, and the size of their brains, the more I believe that what really differentiated home sapiens from other human forms, was that we made friends with some wolves, they didn't, and this relationship became a game changer.

There are different studies which place the origin of the dog in the mid-east, in China, in Europe and Russia. Isn't it likely that this indicates that dogs did not simply emerge in one area, but rather that the similarity between human and wolf family structures, and the fact that our nomadic ancestors were primarily meat eaters, made the union of wolf and man likely to occur in multiple places?

Neanderthals, by Charles R. Knight, 1920, Public Domain

The second fact, the oldest "dog" bones, is a bit shakier, in the sense that collecting, identifying and dating bones depends first on finding them. It's entirely possible that we'll find "dog bones" that go back 50,000 years, etc. There was a wolf which was intentionally buried in Siberia with a human, and in a posture that indicated this was an important animal. The wolf was likely the man's hunting companion.

Having said that, most experts agree that the oldest "dog" bones are about 15,000 years old, which when you're studying evolution and natural selection, is like saying that happened last Tuesday! Perhaps whoever judged those skeletal remains to be a dog, probably noticed a narrower skull, shorter femur, etc. But this corresponds to another notable time period called the agricultural revolution.

Capitoline She Wolf suckling Romulus and Remus. Romulus allegedly founded Rome, 13th century, Public Domain.

As we turned more to farming and less hunter gathering, not only did people have to learn all kinds of new tricks to make a living, so did our dogs, who up until that time were basically gray wolves. As we stopped our nomadic wandering, and were more inclined to set up permanent residence, building shelters, growing vegetation, etc., husbandry began, as we gathered those smaller, less dangerous animals we'd reverse engineer through unnatural selection into the animals we today call livestock.

We may have used natural fencing like English hawthorn, still used to divide the great estates in Britain, and in bush form, with its thorns, rather unpleasant to get through, and we probably had the kind of logistical issues you'd associate with raising semi-feral creatures. Let's say, for sake of argument that the clan elders put your family in charge of raising the animals we'd slowly develop into sheep.

When you went into their enclosure, a certain ram would butt you. That's the one we'll have for dinner. Another ram licked your face. That's the one we'll be breeding. But you still have the problem of scary wild predators, so you go to your dogs, who are just gray wolves, and ask whether any would be willing to guard the sheep, and all paws go in the air. But you can't eat any of the sheep, because that would ruin the economy, so all paws go down.

Seriously, is it possible that the development of dogs out of wolves meant discovering which wolves could overcome their natural inclination to eat the sheep, since they'll be fed mutton around the campfire anyway?

Then as you and your "shepherd dog" get too old, you find out that Barney Rubble, two valleys over, has a "sheep herding" wolf of the opposite gender, and a process of breeding wolves with like skills over thousands of years results in dogs we call the working breeds.

As dogs transitioned from being working members of the family, to pets, meaning surrogates whose only utility was helping warm your bed by night and your lap by day, we began an inbreeding explosion of dogs, doing in a few hundred years what natural selection would take tens of thousands of years to do, which is why thoroughbred dogs have such awful health problems today.

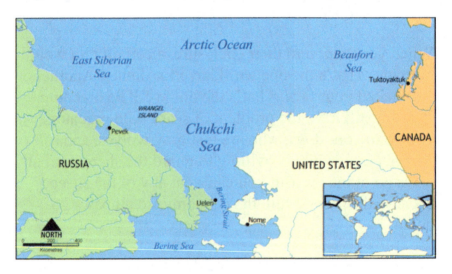

Wrangel Island, public domain, CC BY-SA 3.0, https://commons.wikimedia.org/w/index.php?curid=826115

The critical theory in question has to do with the apparent correlation between mass extinction of large mammals and the arrival of hunter-gatherers in their area. When scientists construct the timeline of man's arrival in the New World, across the Bering Land Bridge, there is a troubling correlation with the arrival of man, and the disappearance of large mammals. One school of thought says that we hunted them to extinction, while over-harvesting seeds, fruits and berries in one area, and then, having exhausted the local ecosystem, moved on. Large predators like big cats and bears, would go extinct because we eliminated their prey.

In all fairness, there is a second theory which says that the disappearance of wildflowers, and other critical vegetation, due to the climate change of that period, was the culprit, eliminating the large mammals, whose predators followed suit. Perhaps it was a combination of both factors.

Still, I struggle with the first theory, mainly because it seems so improbable. I'm sure our ancestors were great hunters. When hunting is not a hobby, but your only means of support, you become proficient, or you starve. Still, eliminating large mammals like mammoths, mastodons and wooly rhinos, with spears, slings and arrows? It's hard to believe that we'd take on such obviously dangerous animals unless we had help.

Similarly, how much success would we have hunting herd animals without help? It's not like we'd reliably find cliffs and canyons whenever we wanted to stampede animals to their deaths or corral them for safer hunting. Quite often, we'd have to use only our paltry weapons and our wits. Harassing wolves, running through herds, and isolating vulnerable elk, for example, would have been a huge help.

One possible clue that we were indeed the culprits is Wrangel Island above Beringia, which was sea-locked after the glacial retreat, and was not invaded by early man. Mammoths lasted on Wrangel Island at least six thousand years after they had disappeared in Alaska.

Why do Dogs and Wolves Look so Different?

So, why do dogs, which cover a bewildering variety of shapes and sizes, look very different from wolves? In 1959, Russian scientist Dmitri Belyayev, began a famous experiment at a silver fox farm, where the unfortunate animals were raised for furs. Belyayev began isolating foxes who showed less fear and aggression with people, and began breeding them to each other. Over many years and many generations, Belyayev's foxes had functionally developed into small dogs, complete with floppy ears and curly tails.

One of the obvious problems of working with wolves, are that these are animals that can hurt you. Wolves have a crushing power of 773 lbs. per square inch in their jaws, about twice that of a German shepherd, because only the most successful jaws got to hunt and eat, and only those wolves survived to hunt again. Only special breeds, like pit bulls, can match wolves in bite strength.

Here's where "unnatural selection" comes in. Our ancestors noticed that wolves are like people, some are taller, larger, smaller, have longer or shorter legs, not to mention different abilities. A wolf pack is not only a family, but a team, with different wolves specializing in different activities, and having differing skill sets. Our ancestors picked up on this, and began to selectively breed, where possible, different wolves to get different looks. If you want a wolf which looks less threatening, you mate two wolves who have shorter snouts, a more pushed-in face, smaller teeth, and more rounded skulls, etc.

Over the last two hundred years, there was an explosion of special breeding. Up until then, wolves, and later, dogs, had been work animals, shepherds, watch dogs, hunting companions, etc.

There's a great scene in the old Disney version of "White Fang", in which the Ethan Hawk character is upbraided by the Tlingit chief for trying to pet White Fang. "We make stones fly, build fires. We are their Gods. He is a worker, not a pet." Victorians discovered that dogs could be lap dogs, or even a substitute for children. The AKC lists over 400 dogs, but three fourths of them are less than two hundred years old.

To sum up, it is possible that man's long history with dogs, is largely a history with wolves, the first domesticated animal.

Great sources for more information: Mark Derr: "How the Dog Became the Dog"; Temple Grandin, "Animals in Translation"; Alexandra Horowitz, "The Inside of a Dog"; Nicholas Wade, "Before the Dawn"; Wolfgang

Schleider and Michael Shalter, "Co-Evolution of Humans and Canids" (PDF on line); "Dogs Decoded" on Nova; and about a dozen books on Wolves and Trophic Cascades, at our web site, http://www.adirondackwildlife.org/Wolf_Frolic_April_20 10.html.

3 FEDERAL LAND, RANCHING & PREDATORS

Western ranchers represent a small fraction of the people living in western states, and the ranchers who graze their livestock on public lands are themselves a minority among ranchers, but they wield a virtual stranglehold on the 250 million acres of federal lands, ranging from BLM lands to US Forest Service lands, to US Fish and Wildlife lands. By itself BLM lands comprise 265 million acres, and ranchers graze livestock on 165 million of those acres. These politically connected ranchers pay the government (through a cost per "animal unit") ***less than fifteen percent*** of the fair market price they'd pay if they leased privately owned lands.

The damage caused by trampled vegetation, soil erosion, and its consequent stream destruction and water pollution, has a devastating impact on the land, not to mention the removal or exclusion of native animals, such as wild horses, bison, elk, deer, bear, prairie dogs, coyotes, wolves, cougars, etc. Most people are not aware of the fact that it is much more efficient to raise cattle east of the Mississippi, which averages much more rain, such that a rancher in Nevada, for example, needs 230 acres annually to support one cow, while those in New York, Vermont, Mississippi and Missouri need only one acre.

Feral horses in Simpson Park area of Nevada managed by the BLM. Public Domain, by the BLM.

Then there is the matter of government subsidies beyond the below market rates the taxpayer realizes when the land is rented for grazing. Why, at a time when we are being told that the government is broke, does Wildlife Services, a seemingly unaccountable unit of the USDA, spend millions of taxpayer dollars every year to kill predators on federal land, which specifically benefits ranchers, who appear to be unfamiliar with the phrase, "the cost of doing business"?

To make matters worse, methods of killing are not restricted to shooting predators on the ground, or by the staggeringly expensive shooting from aircraft, but extend to traps and poisons, which may target predators, but invariably kill pets and other non-target animals, including some of the livestock who accidentally trigger such devices, as well as those predators involved in natural rodent control, such as birds of prey.

Why do "open range laws" in many Western states allow ranchers to let their cattle roam free, and why is it up to the average citizen to fence in their property to prevent destruction by free ranging cattle? If your vehicle strikes a cow which has wandered onto a highway in an open range state like Idaho, you are responsible for both the damage to the cow and to your vehicle.

Small ranchers tend to be conscientious citizens, following good neighbor policies, and are guilty of nothing more than trying to make a living by continuing a family tradition in a business where profitability, as in many other modern business models, is increasingly tied to consolidation, growth and cost cutting. In fact, the reality is that most small farms and ranches in today's economy are run by folks with supplementary job incomes, who struggle to make ends meet.

Most of the taxpayer borne subsidies noted above, accrue to the largest western ranch operators. Of the 18,000 BLM permittees, for example, the top 500 control nearly 50% of the land allocated for grazing. About 30% of all livestock graze mainly part time on these federal lands, while 70% graze exclusively on private lands.

These largest and most politically connected ranchers are often among the most conservative political voters in the country, and the first to brand other folks as "socialists". Right leaning media has done an effective job of frightening many of their followers, by blurring the distinction not only between communism and socialism, for folks who wouldn't know Karl Marx from Groucho Marx, but more importantly, between socialism and a social democracy, which latter best describes the United States, where almost all social services from police to public schools, and from the interstate highway system to our armed forces, are examples of socialism at work. They may say that they do not want "socialism", but *the last thing these big ranchers want is actual capitalism"*.

Cliven & Ammon Bundy speaking at forum hosted by American Academy for Constitutional Education (AAFCE) at the Burke Basic School, by Gage Skidmore in Mesa, Arizona.

The Bundy Bunch & The Land Grabbers

The reason the feds own so much land out west is that the historical process of gaining land through seizure (from Native Americans, for example), wars and cessions (Spain and Mexico) and purchasing (Mexico, France and Great Britain), was followed by the process of setting up states, ceding lands for homesteading, land grants and sales, a process which slowed down because of the remoteness, inaccessibility and, from a private business perspective, not worth the effort or expense, save for tourism and recreational use of much of these lands.

"Right of way" access to land locked lands, mines and

other privately run enterprises is still a matter of great contention out west. Those screaming for state control of these lands seem to forget that the states would then take on the substantial administrative costs currently borne by the federal taxpayer, which could be hundreds of millions of dollars per state.

But this isn't what the Bundys want. When they pose as "The People", what they want is to exclude other peoples, particularly other races, nationalities, and those of different political persuasions, and they want the lands turned over to their ranching businesses, for free, without any oversight. When they wave the flag, which many of us fought for, and therefore find their posturing really offensive, they are simply using the oldest distraction in the book, patriotism as a symbol of self-interest, and an emotive way of disguising their true intent.

Legally, Cliven Bundy and his sons are thieves, who stole from the American taxpayer, and were supported by right leaning media sources, along with several then presidential candidates, until the senior Bundy began offering embarrassing and unsolicited observations on blacks and other minorities, at one point suggesting that blacks were "better off under slavery". As an amusing example of situational outrage, it is now coming out that the Bundys have availed themselves of several government programs, from small business loans to the grazing permits for which they refuse to pay.

Bundy's reasoning on the federal land question seems to be that he should be allowed to graze his livestock on public lands without cost to him, because his family had done so without paying for decades. The fact that the taxpayer subsidizes eighty five percent of the cost of allowing ranchers ***who do pay grazing fees***, to use the federal lands, is somehow not a factor in Bundy's reasoning, even if it is extremely aggravating to those of us who run successful businesses without any federal or state subsidies.

If you follow such notions to their logical conclusion, we should turn the land back to its original human users, the ancestors of Native Americans, before kicking them all back across the Bering Land Bridge, and turning the continent over to mammoths, horses, bison, elk, bears, coyotes, cougars and wolves.

But such reasoning belongs in comedy, and Bundy's supporters seem unable or unwilling to think through the implications of those positions, and further want to make it appear that ranchers represent "The People", an assertion, just in terms of the number of people employed in ranching, completely ludicrous on its face.

The Livestock Interests and Congress

The final irony is that your congressmen and senators, ever mindful of which political contributions ensure their reelection, do not want you to know where your meat comes from, or which cocktails of antibiotics and hormones your livestock ingested before the resulting junkie steer winds up on your dinner plate. Livestock in America consume four times as many antibiotics as people do, which, along with hormones, allow unnatural growth rates, such that the steer you eat today came to market in only about 14 months, while the steak your parents ate took 4 years to get to the table.

Wolves attacking an aurochs, by Heinrich Harder, 1920, public domain.

All cattle were originally bred from a grass grazing Pleistocene ungulate called aurochs. Perhaps consuming all these antibiotics compensates for the fact that the young steer spends his last five months in severely overcrowded feed lots, eating unnatural cattle food ranging from corn to the actual remains of dead steers, while standing and wallowing in their own feces.

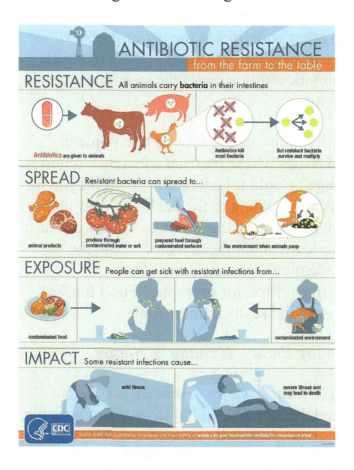

https://www.cdc.gov/foodsafety/from-farm-to-table.html

The greenhouse emissions from livestock raising, chiefly methane, exceed all emissions from trucks and autos combined, but just as Congress has banned using federal funds to study any connection between firearms, violence and crime, so have they made it illegal to use federal funds to collect information on greenhouse gas emissions in raising livestock, and have just recently added meat imported from other countries to the list of products which do not require country of origin labeling, never mind what antibiotics or hormones the steer has ingested, on their packaging.

Ever wonder why politicians want you to completely focus on social issues whose partisan adherence requires only your outrage? Could it be that they're afraid you may discover issues relating to the health of your family and loved ones, never mind the health of Americans as a whole? Want to learn about these issues? Read the "Omnivore's Dilemma", or watch any of the documentaries on Netflix, for example, "Food Inc.", about where your food really comes from.

Healthy Eating, Hunting & Nature

At Adirondack Wildlife, we try to make a practice of never buying unlabeled food, and always, when possible, buying locally grown, naturally raised food. You can't even trust government labels like "organic" and "free range", as their definitions have been so watered down by congress, thanks to relentless lobbying by the food industries, and over the strenuous objections of companies which produce organic foods.

By the time Congress is finished rewarding their major corporate donors, the legal terms "organic" and "free range", have no relation to what you think they mean, and they qualify almost all food as "organic", even when vegetables have had rodenticides and pesticides applied, or in the case of livestock, had antibiotics routinely administered in food and water to all animals, whether they are sick or not, thus encouraging the growth of antibiotic resistant bacteria, which may end up on your plate, if the food itself hasn't been irradiated. Find out specifically where your food comes from and what they've done to it. You can buy free range bison at the grocery store, as well as elk and other wild game online.

We're fortunate living up here in the High Peaks region, as we have natural food stores like Nori's in Saranac Lake, Green Goddess in Lake Placid, Rivermede in Keene Valley, and Rivers Edge in Jay, not to mention many farms and farm stands where we can get fresh vegetables and drug free meat, Ben Wever Farm in Willsboro, Essex farm in Essex, Pray's farm markets in Plattsburgh and Keeseville, Fledging Crow in Keeseville, as well as the Adirondack Buffalo Company in North Hudson, west of exit 29 of the Northway.

Speaking of natural organic meats like venison and elk, if you're in suburbia or rural America, get your hunting license, and harvest some truly wild game, animals which *had a life* outside the feed lot, before being consumed. An odd thing about modern culture, with its emphasis on visual, freeze frame media, rather than reading, or doing what we used to call research: we want to see snippets of life, rather than the process of life, and the more out of the ordinary, the more we prefer it.

We always seem to focus on the ***death*** of the animals we eat, and hardly ever on their ***lives***. We try to humanize the manner in which our livestock are slaughtered, ignoring the fact that for most livestock, particularly chickens and hogs throughout their lives, and cattle for the last 5 months of their lives, living in cramped and severely confined quarters, is the norm, a life consisting of stress and strife. In fact, chickens on huge poultry farms often have their beaks cut off to minimize the damage from the fighting caused by having barely enough room to turn around.

Of course, we also tend to paint an Elysian version of nature, wherein animals prance around the meadows, soaking in that freedom, and living long lives without much stress. For the most part, wild animals don't die of old age. It only seems that way to us, because at the end of a visually and spiritually rewarding day of hiking, fishing or skiing, we go to the kitchen to make dinner, then sit in the hot tub, or before a roaring fire, and sip brandy.

What is strange about our relationship to nature, is that while we absolutely depend on nature (and how we treat her) for our survival as a species, we generally don't experience nature that way on an individual or family basis. We turn on the tap to get water, adjust the thermostat to get heat, and then drive to the market to get food. If we feel ill or become injured, there are doctors, dentists and emergency rooms.

Wildlife do not have any of these options. Most commonly, animals, even the greatest predators, starve, or die because they are starving, and are no longer fast enough to catch prey, escape predation, or strong enough to defend themselves. The bear that wanders into your campsite or back yard after the summer berry crop fails, or the moose suffering from jaw necrosis, who can no longer feed itself, and staggers around waiting for the local wolf pack to smell his disability. Still, no one argues that it would be better for animals to live in zoos.

We caused the explosion of white-tailed deer by exterminating their main source of control, gray wolves. Today, subsistence hunting is the number one cause of mortality among deer, but we kill nearly as many deer with our cars (6 million a year in the U.S.), as do predators, and nearly as many starve to death, particularly in areas where major predators have been removed, and the deer over browse their natural foods, while adapting to eating invasive species, as well as what we grow in that ultimate safe haven, our gardens, where local firearm safety regulations forbid us from discharging weapons so close to houses. But at least wildlife has the experience of freedom, dreadfully challenging though that freedom may sometimes be.

What to do with our Public Lands

Here's a novel thought: why don't we inject a little capitalism into the livestock market, and charge ranchers the fair market value for grazing their animals on public lands, and in those areas where ranchers fail to comply, or choose to no longer use public lands for grazing, allow the natural recovery of the land for use by wildlife and people, allowing American citizens to use those lands for outdoor recreation. This would also improve the setting up of natural safe corridors between wilderness areas like Yellowstone, Glacier, Banff and Jasper, or between Algonquin, the Adirondacks, and Catskill Parks, allowing wildlife to move around between parks, thereby ensuring better health through genetic diversity in our wildlife populations.

The National Parks system has been called the greatest idea anyone ever had, and public visitation in national Parks has seen a steady rise, even during the electronic age, when our kids have their noses buried in games, iPhones and social media.

Expand the National Parks system, and partition public lands for outdoor recreation, be it camping. kayaking, wildlife viewing and photography, four wheeling, snowmobiling, hunting and fishing. *Expanded tourist, sportsman and outdoorsmen revenue generally, would benefit and create entire support communities of restaurants, hotels, outdoor sports equipment stores, naturalist, hunting and fishing guides, etc.*

When ranching dominates an area, you get the opposite, a thin economy with low employment and land devastated by livestock, along with the exclusion of the wildlife. Because the percentage of livestock grazed on public lands is low, and because even these animals tend to be part time grazers, the impact on ranching would be minimal. Oh... and finally shut down the USDA's Wildlife Services, which spends millions to benefit a very small interest group.

The return of wolves to Yellowstone, in the nineties, to control the elk, who were severely over browsing riparian vegetation and impacting a wide range of species from song birds to beaver, created an annual average of over $35 million in additional revenue to Gardiner, West Yellowstone, Silvergate and Cooke City, and other tourist towns surrounding Yellowstone, a fact you will never learn from conservative western media and politicians, who tend to be in the pockets of wealthy ranching and mining interests, and now that Bundy claims he's on a mission from god, he'll get support from all those Americans who seem to forget that all terrorists claim to be "on a mission from god".

4 REWILDING THE ADIRONDACKS

The Adirondacks is the largest park in the lower 48 states, its patchwork quilt of private and public lands so large, you could easily fit Yellowstone, Glacier, and Yosemite inside the Park's 6 million acres. Tourism is a key business in the Adirondacks, with 12.4 % of all jobs related to tourism. At the same time, only $2 out of every hundred spent on tourism in New York State ends up in the Adirondacks. Even granting that 64% ends up in that tourist mecca, the Big Apple, the numbers for the Adirondacks, and the tourist attractions they offer, seem lower than you'd expect.

Most of our Adirondack towns and villages, particularly those outside the High Peaks, Lake George and Old Forge areas, present a challenging environment in which to make a living, and our kids are more likely to leave the Adirondacks for more promising job markets. Some folks say bring back manufacturing, others say build more resorts, still others say "leave it alone, we like it this way, the fewer people and tourists the better". But if we do agree to discuss as a goal, bringing more opportunity to the smaller towns and hamlets within the Park, is there a way to do this that uses current and potential natural resources, such as wildlife?

Wildlife drives tourist revenue

Wildlife helps drive tourist revenue and can therefore help create hospitality and infrastructure support jobs. Wolves were reintroduced to Yellowstone and central Idaho in the mid-90s, not only to rewild Yellowstone, but also in an attempt to better manage the exploding elk herds, and the habitat damages they were causing.

Coywolf on trailcam, Adirondack Wildlife Refuge, by Steve Hall

Lost in the ongoing political screaming from pro-wolf and anti-wolf factions on either side, was an interesting economic development: in data gathered through surveys between 2004 and 2006, it turned out that a high percentage of Yellowstone visitors cited the possibility of seeing wolves, as a major factor in visiting Yellowstone. This translated into an estimated $35 million in extra annual dollars spent in the local economies of Gardiner, West Yellowstone, Silver Gate, Cooke City, and the other Montana and Wyoming towns which border Yellowstone. About 3.5% of Yellowstone visitors claimed they had come *only* to see wolves, and would have gone elsewhere (Banff, Denali, Algonquin, etc.) were there no chance of seeing wolves.

The Regional Office of Sustainable Tourism (ROOST) promotes Adirondack tourism to the traveling public, and releases annual reports, based on surveys of tourists who interact with the visitors' center through walk-ins, call-ins, reach out and social media. Their report in 2014 estimated that these 477,000 tourists spent about 177 million dollars in tourist related activities, such as lodging, dining, shopping, etc., with an average stay of about 5 days, and an average spending rate of about $325 per day.

Hiking is the most popular reported outdoor activity, followed by canoeing and kayaking, skiing and snowboarding, and the ever more popular cycling. Curiously, the only mention of wildlife viewing queried in the survey, are visits to the Adirondack Wildlife Refuge, where visitors went on the "Wolf Walk", to learn about wolves.

Cougar by National Park Service, public domain.

What if ROOST actively promoted wildlife viewing, for example, the possibility of seeing elk, wolves or cougar, as a remote possibility while hiking (wolves and cougar tend to flee), better possibility while canoeing (all mammals come to drink), and a still stronger possibility while driving (most wildlife sightings are of animals crossing roads). What if this emphasis on wildlife tourism resulted in only a 10% increase in tourism? That would be over $16 million dollars, and would not include the majority of tourists, hunters, fishermen, etc. (some seven to ten million!) who come to the Adirondacks each year, without interacting with the tourist bureau. If we included these visitors, and added ten percent, we'd be bringing some $160 million dollars into the economy. These speculative estimates ***do not*** include potential boosts to hotels in convention and meetings bookings.

Ahote, an ambassador black bear at the Adirondack Wildlife Refuge, by Steve Hall

There are success stories about restoring elk to previous habitats where they had been hunted out before the advent of hunting seasons and regulation, such as in Kentucky and western Pennsylvania, where restoration has been so successful, elk have become an important tourist revenue factor, and controlled, seasonal hunting has resumed.

Adirondack megafauna of the past

While the increasing numbers of deer and black bear constitute Adirondack megafauna today, in the not so distant past, the ecosystem of the "forever wild" Adirondacks supported wolves, cougars, lynx, wolverine, moose, elk and wood bison. Today, moose, recovering from a history of unrestricted hunting, probably number a very sparse 400 to 500 animals in New York, and the DEC is engaged in surveys to get a better handle on moose numbers, and whether they are increasing or, following the current trend in Maine, New Hampshire, Vermont, Minnesota and Montana, decreasing.

Studies indicate that potential wolf recovery areas include the Adirondacks and northern New England. At Adirondack Wildlife, we frequently receive photos of "Eastern Coyotes", or what we call "coywolves" from Face Book followers, all asking whether these are "wolves". The coywolf is a wolf-coyote hybrid, and as the accompanying photograph from a trail cam at the Adirondack Wildlife Refuge shows, coywolves are sometimes twice the size of western coyotes, and often *difficult to distinguish from wolves*, especially for a layman who sees one for only a few seconds.

The largest obstacle to wolves returning to the Adirondacks is relentless hunting and trapping of wolves in southern Quebec and Ontario. For our purposes, bolstering the Adirondacks as a place where visitors may see wolves, is it so critical what percentage "wolf" our wolves are, when few visitors can distinguish gray wolves from Canadian wolves from coywolves?

Wandering, transient male cougars occasionally pass through the Adirondacks, but there is no *evidence* of female cougars raising kittens and defending territories anywhere east of Missouri and the Michigan Upper Peninsula. Male Cougars will set up territories when they have sufficient prey, which they do have in the Adirondacks, and female cougars in territories overlapped by their territories.

Unlike the confusion between coywolves and wolves, it's difficult to mistake a cougar for, say, a bobcat or lynx, unless presented with an obscured or partial glimpse. Without reintroducing cougars to the Adirondacks, particularly females, it is unlikely we'll have a breeding population in the Adirondacks.

More than 300 Rocky Mountain Elk were released in the Adirondacks over six years, starting in 1893, but were extirpated by hunting, poaching and the expansion of white-tailed deer, who passed brain worm and round worm to the elk. Other than that experience, mentions of elk are only found historically (a travel editor mentions them in 1836), and in scattered Iroquois and Algonquin references.

Elk in Yellowstone, by Steve Hall

Wood Bison have probably been gone for over 200 years, and I don't believe there have been any specific studies about whether the Adirondacks, logged, cleared, reforested and generally altered over time, would offer suitable browse for elk and grazing for bison.

Lynx are occasionally reported in New York, but as with cougar, there is no evidence yet of breeding and setting up territories, although Sue Morse of Keeping Track has encountered them in northern Vermont. Eighty lynx from northwest Canada were radio collared and released in the Adirondacks, over a three-year period, starting in 1989 and some dispersed up to 400 miles from the release areas.

Unlike the bobcat, which has a more generalized prey base, and whose numbers continue to expand in the Adirondacks, lynx are specialized snowshoe hare predators. Wolverine were last reported in New York in 1840, and their smaller cousins, fishers, are doing well in the Adirondacks, and expanding their ranges in New York State.

Previous reintroductions of megafauna often suffered from lack of funding for follow up.

What went right and wrong with Rewilding in Yellowstone

The ecological benefit of returning a keystone predator to Yellowstone was to restore some natural balance, but politics is never far from any discussions about wildlife and sustainability. In the years since wolf reintroduction, anger over real and imagined consequences of wolves in ranching and hunting country, led state legislatures to cancel the thirty mile no-wolf-hunting buffer zone within the Greater Yellowstone Ecosystem around Yellowstone National Park, and since wolves don't know where the park boundaries lie, their numbers in Yellowstone have been reduced by hunting.

The Congress is more likely to weaken the Endangered Species Act, as well as return more control over wildlife and natural resources to the states. In other words, the positive effects of wolves returning to the Yellowstone ecosystem have been seriously compromised, as has the chances of tourists seeing wolves in Yellowstone. Good discussions about keystone predator effects and the science of "Trophic Cascades" may be found in "The Wolf's Tooth" and "The Carnivore Way", by Cristina Eisenberg.

Wood Bison, US Fish and Wildlife, Public Domain

The big picture

Hunting, as reflected in the annual purchase of hunting licenses, is declining in the U.S. for many reasons, including habitat destruction, and less hunter free time for often more distant hunting access. More importantly, from a cultural perspective, our children and grandchildren are growing up in the digital age, and for many, what little interaction they have with nature is through electronic devices, video games and media.

Most significantly, the earth has lost 40% of its wildlife over the past 50 years, and appears to be in a period scientists are calling the sixth extinction. Unlike previous mass extinctions, this one seems to be driven by the direct impact of an exploding human population, with its critical hallmarks being habitat destruction, over exploitation of our resources, pollution, poaching, invasive species and disease. We seem to have lost sight of the fact that nature may be "entertaining", but we are also a part of nature, and we despoil it at our peril, even as we deny doing so.

Yellowstone of the East?

Does all this mean that we could turn the Adirondacks into the Yellowstone of the East, by rewilding megafauna? Well, not exactly. First of all, from a wildlife perspective, much of the allure of Yellowstone is its wide-open vistas, meaning it's much easier to spot large animals, while the Adirondacks is more characterized by mixtures of thick conifer and deciduous forest. As in many forested wildlife environments, when you hike in the Adirondacks, critters tend to hear you, see you or smell you, and flee before your approach, which is why you're more likely to see wildlife while canoeing, or surprise wildlife while driving.

There is a much better model for a rewilded Adirondacks, and that is Algonquin Provincial Park in Ontario, about two hundred ninety miles northwest of

Lake Placid. Both parks are part of the Southern Canadian Shield and are generally characterized as Eastern Boreal transition ecoregions. The Adirondacks has mountains, while Algonquin features rugged and rocky hills, but both have many lakes and waterways, and both are visually inspiring.

Algonquin forms a wildlife corridor with the Adirondacks, and comprises the northern end of an important gene exchange with the Adirondacks, mixing gene pools, as animals wander back and forth between ecosystems, just as the Adirondacks forms such a corridor with the Catskills and Appalachians. One of the most important challenges for parks and wildlife refuges is the dangers of genetic isolation, which impacts diversity within a species, or as we put it at the Refuge, "The key to wildlife survival is connected habitat". It is in the interests of both these parks to restrict trapping in the corridor between them, to allow the flow of genes back and forth.

Algonquin has populations of Eastern Canadian wolves, deer, beaver, and may be the surest place in North America to see moose. This last is because the 35 miles of Highway 60 runs through the southern end of the park, and is bordered by many bogs, beaver ponds and meadows, which attract moose at various times of year. Algonquin is also the only park I've visited, besides Yellowstone, where I've seen wolves multiple times.

Curiously, Highway 60 is somewhat mirrored by Route 3 in the Adirondacks. Picture, in particular, that sparsely populated, 40-mile-long stretch of Route 3 between Tupper Lake and Star Lake, and like Highway 60, passes through areas where the forest is interrupted by lakes, bogs and beaver ponds, or the stretch between Paul Smith and Malone, or Tupper Lake and Old Forge.

The secret to successful wildlife tourism is often not only what you are very likely to see, but what you believe you *may* see. Imagine if we add to the various reasons to visit the Adirondacks, wildlife viewing, the outside chance of seeing a moose browsing in a beaver bog, or hearing a bull elk bugling in a meadow, or a wolf or cougar crossing the road. Even if we had cougar and wolf, the chances of seeing them in, say, the High Peaks area, would be very low, as there are fewer deer there, and too many people. If you're staying at one of the large hotels in Lake Placid, where according to ROOST, most Essex County lodging dollars are spent, you may decide to take that picturesque drive from Saranac Lake through Tupper Lake, and on towards Watertown.

You may discover there is more wildlife off the beaten path between Tupper Lake and Star Lake, but if you wish to grab a room to stay in the area for a day or so, so that you can go out with your camera at dawn or dusk (always the best time to see wildlife), you'll find limited facilities. Or, to look at it from the inn keeper's perspective, let's say you're running a small motel or BnB in Tupper Lake,

Cranberry Lake or Star Lake, and you add to that list of amenities on Trip Advisor, Home Away or Air BnB, wildlife viewing, featuring photographs of wildlife, taken by your guests.

Zeebie at Adirondack Wildlife Refuge, by Jesse Gigandet

What if you are a hunting or fishing guide, and you're operating out in the wildlife rich, Cranberry Lake area? You already know that your deer hunters are not patronizing you because they'll have more deer to target. We tease visitors who come to the Adirondacks to hunt deer, about the fact that there are very likely more deer where they live than here, and they always respond the same way: "We're here *because* it's the Adirondacks". What if you add to the list of hunt and release creatures wolf and cougar? What hunter/ hiker/ fisherman wouldn't be thrilled to see, never mind photograph either?

A rewilded Adirondacks would have a major tourist advantage over Algonquin. While Algonquin is only about a four-hour drive from Toronto and three hours from Ottawa, the Adirondacks is within driving range of the much more populous New York, Buffalo, Boston, Albany, Hartford, Burlington and Montreal metro areas, and has a more robust hospitality infrastructure. In addition, access to Algonquin is remote, and once you're within 100 miles of the east or west gates, you're on two lane roads.

This article is not about **whether** rewilding will work in the Adirondacks, and there are a number of additional issues to discuss, which I'll tackle in subsequent articles, such as, how will rewilding impact sheep and cattle ranching, are wolves and cougars dangerous to people, and will this impact the behavior of deer towards hunters?

There are a number of non-profits currently working on rewilding, with habitat specialists and biologists taking a fresh look at an old topic, because they have learned much more about our habitat and its carrying capacity for wildlife, and like many others, they view the preservation of the wild as a legacy and a duty. They also see what is happening on the Federal level and are thinking this may be an opportunity for visionary business, civic and both state and local political leaders, to examine a potential broadening of the Adirondack economy, and step up to promote a real return to "Forever Wild".

Wolves, Humans, Dogs & Civilization

ABOUT THE AUTHOR

Steve and Wendy Hall are cofounders and owners of Adirondack Wildlife Refuge in Wilmington, NY. We've rehabbed wild animals for 45 years and conducted education seminars on Nature and its critters for 20 years. Wendy, who was not only a wildlife rehabber, but a very accomplished artist, died at seventy in January of 2022 of an inoperable sarcoma. Other books by Steve Hall include "Owls of the Adirondacks" and "Tooth and Claw- Adirondack Mammals".

Made in the USA
Columbia, SC
28 August 2023